An Adult Christ at Christmas

Raymond E. Brown, s.s.

Com OJS
Menlo Park
CA.

An Adult Christ at Christmas

Essays on the
Three Biblical Christmas Stories
Matthew 2 and Luke 2

The Liturgical Press
Collegeville, Minnesota

The essays reprinted here were originally published in *Worship* (under the usual rules of ecclesiastical approbation) as follows:
"The Meaning of the Magi . . . ," 49 (December 1975) 574–582.
"The Meaning of the Manger . . . ," 50 (November 1976) 528–538.
"The Presentation of Jesus . . . ," 51 (January 1977) 2–11.
"The Finding of the Boy Jesus . . . ," 51 (November 1977) 474–485.

Cover design by Mary Jo Pauly

11	12	13	14	15

Brown, Raymond Edward.
    An adult Christ at Christmas : essays on the three Biblical Christmas stories—Matthew 2 and Luke 2 / Raymond E. Brown.
        p.   cm.
    ISBN 0-8146-0997-X (pbk.)
    1. Bible. N.T. Matthew II, 1-23—Criticism, interpretation, etc. 2. Bible. N.T. Luke II—Criticism, interpratation, etc. 3. Jesus Christ—Nativity. I. Title.
BS2575.2.B758 1988
226'.06—dc19   88-9046
                                                   CIP

Contents

Foreword

In October 1977 my full-scale commentary on the infancy narratives in Matthew and Luke, entitled *The Birth of the Messiah*, was published by Doubleday (Garden City, New York). Almost a decade of my life and work went into that commentary, and as it was nearing completion I was eager to share with readers some of the insights I had gained. Consequently, in 1975 I began to publish in the Christmas-season issues of *Worship* a series of popular essays dealing with the implications of my work — a plan which continued in 1976 and 1977. Now that the commentary has been published, for scholarly purposes it supplants these short essays. And yet in conversation with the editors of *Worship* I became convinced that it might serve a twofold purpose to make these Christmas essays available in a booklet.

First, *The Birth of the Messiah* is a long work (600 pages); and even though it is written so that large parts of it can be useful to any educated reader, it has scholarly aspects which many would find formidable. For such readers this booklet may serve as an introduction to *The Birth of the Messiah*. In a much more popular form they can sample the approach that I use and get a feeling for the method and conclusions. Indeed, this booklet may serve as a text in study clubs where the leader would have worked through *The Birth of the Messiah*.

Second, even many of those who have read the long commentary may not see immediately how to present its contents in a simpler way to others. I think particularly of preachers who wish to incorporate the contents of *The Birth of the Messiah* into their sermons. The essays in this booklet may help them as examples of how to pick out what is more important. There is material for fifty sermons in the long commentary; but the topics I have chosen in these essays touch on sections most appropriate for Christmas, and that in itself may be a help to interested clergy and teachers.

Because the original essays in *Worship* were written over a period of three years, I had to repeat from one to the other some basic attitudes toward christology and gospel composition. This republication of the essays has enabled me to eliminate the repetition and to gather together in an Introduction my fundamental presuppositions. This rearrangement of the material should make the whole more readable and cogent. Nevertheless, I resisted the temptation to introduce into the essays much new material; I have written one book on the subject and I have no wish to write it all over again in order to fill out a booklet.

I am grateful to the editors of *Worship* for cooperating with me in this project of enabling a wider audience to profit from the fruits of the modern scientific (critical) approach to the infancy narratives. Their interest reassures me in my basic conviction that such a study of the Bible is not for the few but is beneficial to the many, both for their spiritual life and for their comprehension of the liturgy.

Union Theological Seminary, New York City
Feast of the Presentation of the Lord, 2 February 1978

An Adult Christ at Christmas

Introduction

On Putting an Adult Christ Back into Christmas

The Gospels of Matthew and Luke begin with stories of Jesus' conception and birth (henceforth called infancy narratives). In this they differ notably from the other two Gospels which tell us nothing of Jesus' family origins; indeed, Mark does not even mention Joseph, while John never gives the name of the mother of Jesus. The Matthean and Lucan infancy narratives, which are not at all alike, have supplied the raw material for the Christmas feast so dear to Christians. How are we to evaluate them?

The Roman Catholic Church, often thought to be painfully conservative in its official positions, has issued a rather liberal pronouncement on the general historicity of the Gospels. Through its official organ for biblical teaching,[1] Rome has insisted that one should speak of the Gospels as historical in the sense that the four accounts of the ministry of Jesus took their origin in words that Jesus spoke and deeds that he performed. Nevertheless, the pronouncement made clear that those words and deeds underwent considerable adaptation from the time of Jesus' ministry until the time when they were written down in the Gospels.[2] For instance, there was a

[1] I refer to the Pontifical Biblical Commission which issued its Instruction on *The Historical Truth of the Gospels* in 1964. A full English translation and commentary was given by J. A. Fitzmyer, *Theological Studies* 25 (1964) 386–408. The most important sections of the Instruction appear in an appendix of my book *Biblical Reflections on Crises Facing the Church* (New York: Paulist 1975).

[2] The Instruction distinguishes "three stages of tradition by which the doctrine and life of Jesus have come down to us." Stage one, the ministry of Jesus,

Adult Christology

1

period of oral transmission wherein the apostles preached what Jesus had said and done; but they infused their accounts of Jesus with a post-resurrectional insight into his divinity — an insight they had not had when he was alive.[3] Then, in the commission to writing by the evangelists[4] there was a further selection, synthesis and explication of the accounts that had come down from apostolic preaching with the result that the final Gospel narratives of the ministry are not necessarily literal accounts of what Jesus did and said. As the Roman document affirmed, "The truth of the story is not at all affected by the fact that the Evangelists relate the words and deeds of the Lord in a different order and express his sayings not literally but differently, while preserving their sense."

Unfortunately most Roman Catholics, including many clergy and religion teachers, do not know this official position about the Gospels taken by their Church, so that there is still uneasiness if someone argues that a particular section dealing with Jesus' ministry is not literal history. Consequently, before any Catholic turns to a serious study of the infancy narratives, he or she should become familiar with the Roman Biblical Com-

certainly belongs to the first third of the first century A.D. (*ca*. 28–30). Stage two, the period of apostolic preaching, can plausibly be dated to the second third of the century (*ca*. 30–65) since the best-known apostles were dead by the mid-60s. Stage three, the period of Gospel writing, can reasonably be dated to the last third of the century (probably Mark in the late 60s; Matthew and Luke in the 70s or 80s; John in the late 80s or 90s).

[3] The Instruction (VIII) speaks of Jesus' divinity being perceived after he rose from the dead.

[4] The Instruction distinguishes between the apostles who preached and the sacred authors who composed their Gospels from what had been handed down in this preaching. This corresponds to the general scholarly position today that no one of the Gospels was written by an eyewitness to the ministry of Jesus. An earlier position, reflected in Biblical Commission decrees at the beginning of the twentieth century, that Matthew and John were written by members of the Twelve (something never claimed by the Gospels themselves) has been almost universally abandoned, as tacitly acknowledged in 1955 by the Secretary of the Commission who gave Catholics "complete freedom" with regard to such previous decrees.

Introduction

mission's approach to the Gospels in general. One will never understand the infancy narratives without first being convinced that, in the course of transmission from Jesus to the evangelists, all Gospel material has been colored by the faith and experience of the Church of the first century.

The next step in approaching the infancy narratives is the recognition that the Instruction of the Biblical Commission about the Gospels does *not* cover the birth stories,[5] for it concerns only what Jesus said and did *during his ministry* — words and deeds witnessed by apostles who subsequently passed them on. (No one has ever suggested that such apostolic witnesses as Peter and John were around for the events at Bethlehem.) If one wishes to discuss the infancy material, one must extend even farther the liberal attitude of the Commission about historicity. That is why I claim that for many people the narratives of Jesus' birth and infancy constitute "the last frontier" to be crossed in gaining an appreciation of the implications of a modern scientific (critical) approach to the New Testament. In this short collection of essays from *Worship* I would like to see if I can make this frontier seem less a barrier.

One way to assist readers in crossing the frontier is by acquainting them with previous attempts in this direction, for in a certain sense readers must work through in their own minds the kinds of questions that have been asked in the history of scholarship about the infancy narratives. They are basic questions and there is no way to avoid them.

At the risk of oversimplification, I would say that scholarship on the infancy narratives has passed through two stages and is entering a third. The first stage was one of recognizing the im-

[5] The Commission was aware of this, for after 1964 there was a movement to issue a second statement pertaining to the infancy narratives. This attempt was abandoned after the consultors were asked for their advice — probably because the Cardinals who composed the Commission thus came face to face with the enormous difficulties to be encountered in pronouncing on the historicity of the infancy narratives.

Adult Christology

portance of the distinction mentioned above, namely, that the birth material had a different origin from the material concerning Jesus' ministry. Our knowledge of the substance of the ministry came from apostolic testimony; but we simply do not know whose testimony, if anyone's, supported a story like that of the magi and the star. There was a tendency to posit family testimony (of Joseph and Mary) underlying the infancy stories, but that was simply a guess.

And that guess became more and more difficult to sustain as scholarship moved into the second stage, involving biblical criticism of the infancy stories taken separately from the rest of the Gospel. There was the overall striking fact that Matthew and Luke tell two very different stories of Jesus' birth and infancy — stories that agree in very few details [6] and almost contradict one another in other details. [7] A complicating factor was the impossibility of substantiating some of the startling events which should have attracted public notice — for example, a star that moved through the heavens in a totally irregular way but left no astronomical record. [8] The resulting doubts about his-

[6] Albeit very important details, such as the birth at Bethlehem and the virginal conception.

[7] The most notorious discrepancy is between Matthew's account of a flight to Egypt in face of Herod's persecution, and Luke's account of a peaceful return to Nazareth through Jerusalem without the slightest involvement of Herod. A perceptive reading shows that Matthew thinks that the home of Mary and Joseph was in Bethlehem (2:11), so that he has to explain why, when they came back from Egypt, they went to Nazareth instead of to Bethlehem (2:22–23); for Luke, they came from Nazareth in the first place.

[8] There are unverifiable (and even unlikely) historical statements as well, such as the Herodian slaughter of the children at Bethlehem, and the universal census of the Roman Empire under Augustus (involving Herod's kingdom!). There have been many ingenious attempts to "prove" these as facts — unsuccessful in my judgment. For instance, there was a remarkable conjunction of planets in 7–6 B.C., and Halley's comet appeared in 12–11 B.C. But Matthew describes a star — in fact, a star that came to rest over the place where Jesus was. If one wishes to invoke astronomy to explain Matthew 2, one should recognize the probable direction of the ancient thought pattern. *After* people came to believe in the risen Jesus as the Son of God, in retrospect they would

Introduction

4

toricity were aggravated when it was recognized that the infancy stories echo Old Testament stories to an extent unparal-
leled in the rest of the Gospels. They were sometimes conceived to have arisen through meditation on Old Testament
motifs, a process to which the name *midrash* was frequently
applied (and not always with a real understanding of *midrash*).
Were the essays in this booklet written during that second stage
of scholarship, they might have been entitled: "Were There
Magi? Was There a Star? Was There a Census? Did Angels
Appear to Shepherds?"

But we are now entering a third and much more positive
stage of investigation. Without neglecting the historical problems uncovered in the previous stage, scholars have turned
their attention to the theology of the infancy narratives. What-
ever their origin or historicity,[9] why were these stories included
by Matthew and Luke in their Gospels? How does each infancy
narrative accord with the respective evangelist's theology?
How do the infancy narratives convey the good news of salvation, so that they are truly and literally "gospel"? Such questions are my real interest in these essays, as I have tried to
indicate in two of the titles by speaking of meaning and significance. The answer to them can play a role in proclamation
to the Christian community.

Let me turn here to the first of the above questions: Why
were these stories deemed appropriate by Matthew and Luke
to be included in their Gospels? In the period before the application of biblical criticism this question would not have been
asked: the Gospels were looked on as biographies of Jesus, and
so it would have been only common sense to include material

begin to look for an astronomical phenomenon to associate with the birth of
such a figure — and the result may have been a combination of vague
memories of astronomical phenomena in the period 12–6 B.C. with the Old
Testament imagery of the Davidic star (see below).

[9] In *The Birth of the Messiah* I devote the necessary attention to questions of
historicity, but I deliberately place such questions last lest they get out of focus.

Adult Christology

about the birth of Jesus. But now we have come to recognize that the Gospels are not primarily biographical in their origins; rather they stem from an apostolic preaching where salvific import determined what was preserved about Jesus.

The oldest preaching concerned the salvific action par excellence — that is, the death and resurrection of Jesus; and so the passion narrative was the oldest part of the gospel tradition. To the passion narrative (and thus in a process that worked chronologically backwards) were eventually joined collections of sayings and healings, precisely because in the light of the resurrection the true salvific import of such memories of the ministry of Jesus became clear. It is noteworthy that the most ancient evangelist, Mark, called the baptism of Jesus "The beginning of the gospel of Jesus Christ": the beginning of the gospel was equated with the beginning of the preaching of the kingdom. Clearly Mark's interests were not biographical; indeed, he tells us nothing of Jesus' origins.[10]

Having discarded biographical completeness as the primary motive, we then have to ask why Matthew and Luke moved the beginning of the gospel of Jesus Christ from the baptism back to the conception. The answer lies in the christological significance that they saw in the conception and birth. For them, not the baptism but the conception and birth constituted the moment when God revealed who Jesus was. Let me sketch briefly the chronologically backwards-growth in the first-century Christian understanding of this "christological moment." In the ancient preaching the moment of God's revealing the christological identity of Jesus was the resurrection-exaltation:[11] "This Jesus God raised up. . . . God made him

[10] Mark does not show favor to Jesus' natural family; it is firmly replaced by a true family consisting of disciples (3:31–35, especially when read in sequence to 3:19–21, where "his own" think Jesus is frenzied). Thus, the recent suggestion of M. Miguens that Mark does not mention Joseph because he wants his readers to know that Jesus was virginally conceived is implausible; see note 59 below.

[11] A still earlier christology, leaving only faint traces in the New Testament, may have made the parousia the christological moment: Jesus would be the

Introduction

both Lord and Messiah, this Jesus whom you crucified" (Acts 2:32, 36; also 5:31). We hear in Acts 13:33 that by raising Jesus from the dead, God fulfilled his words in Psalm 2:7: "You are my son; today I have begotten you." As the Christian creedal statement quoted by Paul in Romans 1:4 phrases it: by resurrection from the dead Jesus was designated Son of God in power according to the Spirit of holiness (the Holy Spirit). Such a concentration on the resurrection as the christological moment was consonant with the earliest stage in gospel formation, which, as I mentioned above, centered on the death and resurrection of Jesus.

As more attention was focused on Jesus' ministry and on his Galilean proclamation of the kingdom through words and mighty deeds, the emphasis on the resurrection as the moment when Jesus was "made Lord" and "begotten" or "designated" as God's Son was seen as inadequate. It did not do justice to the continuity between the Jesus of the ministry and the risen Lord. Christian penetration of the mystery of Jesus illuminated the fact that he was already Lord and Messiah during his lifetime, so that the resurrection was the unveiling of a divine sonship that was already there. Thus, for the oldest written Gospel, Mark, the christological moment has moved from the resurrection to the baptism, where Jesus is designated by divine revelation as God's Son. The Holy Spirit, which in early Christian experience was associated with the risen Jesus, now descends on him at the baptism and remains with him during his ministry.[12]

But this development in Christian understanding[13] still left

Messiah, the Son of Man, when he would return again — a *possible* interpretation of Acts 3:20–21.

[12] The themes present in a creedal statement like Romans 1:4 appear in narrative form in Mark 1:10–11 and Luke 3:22; 4:14 (designation as Son; Holy Spirit; power). The Western text of Luke 3:22 ("You are my son; today I have begotten you") applies to the baptism the same psalm passage that Acts 13:33 applies to the resurrection.

[13] Let me stress that I am speaking of a development in the understanding of a reality that was already there. This approach is quite different from the liberal

Adult Christology

unsolved the question of whether the baptism was the moment when Jesus *became* God's Son. Was the heavenly voice adopting Jesus? Such a misunderstanding is ruled out by the prefixing of infancy narratives in Matthew and Luke, narratives which make clear that Jesus was God's Son during his whole earthly life, from the moment of his conception through the Holy Spirit. The divine declaration of sonship, once attached to the resurrection and then to the baptism, is now attached by an "angel of the Lord" [14] to the conception of Jesus in the womb of the Virgin Mary. [15] This declaration makes it clear that the child is the Messiah, "the king of the Jews" (Mt 2:2), "a Savior who is the Messiah and Lord" (Lk 2:11). And so the story of Jesus' conception is no longer just an item of popular biography; it is the vehicle of the good news of salvation; in short, it is gospel. Reflection on how this came about will explain to readers why I have entitled this Introduction: "On Putting an Adult Christ *Back* into Christmas." The process was literally an interpretative one of reading back later insights into the birth stories, and those later insights involved an adult Christ who had died and risen.

Both in Matthew and in Luke the *first* chapter of the Gospel narrates the story of the conception of Jesus with the accompanying revelation of who he is. The essays that follow in my little book concern the *second* chapter of each Gospel — the Christmas story of the birth at Bethlehem of the child who has been conceived in Mary's womb. Why is this also gospel? The answer to this question lies in the historical aftermath of the

thesis that Christians created *ex nihilo* a christology by making Jesus the Son of God. See the survey of modern scholarship on gospel christology that constitutes chapter 2 of my *Biblical Reflections on Crises Facing the Church* (note 1 above).

[14] The classic Old Testament image for the revealing God.

[15] In the light of Romans 1:4 (and note 12 above), notice the phraseology of the divine revelation in Luke 1:35: "The *Holy Spirit* will come upon you, and the *power* of the Most High will overshadow you; therefore the child to be born *will be called* holy, the *Son of God*."

Introduction

revelation of the good news of salvation — a revelation that, as we have seen, was once attached to the resurrection. After the resurrection of Jesus the apostles went forth and *proclaimed* that good news, first to Jews and then to Gentiles. This proclamation was met by a twofold *response*: some believed and came to worship the exalted Lord Jesus; others rejected both the message and the preachers. When the evangelists looked back into the life of Jesus with post-resurrectional hindsight, they could see the same sequence after the baptism of Jesus (which had become an earlier moment of the revelation of who he was). Jesus *proclaimed* the good news of the kingdom throughout Galilee and this led to a twofold *response*: some drew close to him and became his disciples; others rejected him and came to hate him. And so when the evangelists told stories of the conception of Jesus attaching the revelation of Jesus' identity to that moment of his life, they tended to follow the sequence once more. In the second chapter of each infancy narrative we hear how the good news was *proclaimed* to others and how that proclamation met a twofold *response*. Let us turn now to the way in which the sequence is narrated in each Gospel, with the hope that in our own lives the recognition that there is an adult message about Christ in Christmas will lead us to proclaim that revelation to others that they too may respond in faith.

Adult Christology

The First Christmas Story (Matthew 2:1–23)

The Meaning of the Magi; the Significance of the Star

The evangelist tells the story of the magi and the star after he has already given the genealogy of Jesus and told how an angel announced to Joseph in a dream the forthcoming birth of the child who would be the Davidic Messiah (see 1:1, 16, 18), a child conceived through the Holy Spirit and therefore the Son of God (see also 2:15).

For brevity's sake, let me simply list scholarly observations about the parts of the Matthean infancy narrative that supply a *framework* for the story of the magi and the star:

1. In the annunciation to Joseph, Matthew follows the pattern of the typical annunciation of birth in the Old Testament — for example, of the births of Isaac (Gn 17:15–21) and of Samson (Jgs 13).[16]

2. Matthew's portrayal of Joseph who receives revelation in dreams (1:20; 2:13, 19) and who goes down to Egypt (2:14) resembles the portrait of Joseph in the Old Testament, the patriarch who was "the dreamer" par excellence (Gn 37:19 — literally, "the master of dreams") and who went down to Egypt, escaping an attempt on his life (Gn 37:28).

3. Matthew's account of Jesus' escape from Herod is remarkably like the Jewish story of Moses' escape from the Pharaoh — the Moses who, like Jesus, came back from the Egypt to which Joseph had gone. The biblical narrative of Moses' birth had un-

---

[16] The annunciation pattern for the birth of Jesus is found also in Luke and was presumably developed in popular circles anterior to both written Gospels, each of which uses the pattern in its own way.

First Christmas Story

dergone considerable popular expansion by the first century
A.D., as we can see in writers of that period like Philo and
Josephus. In the expanded narrative Pharaoh was forewarned
through his scribes (see Mt 2:4) that a child was about to be
born who would prove a threat to his crown, and so he and his
advisers decided to kill all the Hebrew male children. At the
same time, through a dream there was divine revelation to
Moses' father that his wife, already pregnant, would bear the
child who would save Israel, a child who would escape
Pharaoh's massacre. Forewarned, the parents acted to preserve
the life of Moses when he was born. Later in life, Moses fled
into Sinai and returned only when he heard from the Lord:
"All those who were seeking your life are dead" (Ex 4:19; cf.
Mt 2:20).

The story of the magi and the star also echoes the Pentateu-
chal account of Moses but combines this with the imagery of a
Messiah descended from David — an imagery for which Matthew has prepared us by beginning the infancy narrative with
"the genealogy of Jesus Christ, the son of David." The Pen-
tateuchal passage is Numbers 22–24, the episode involving
Balaam. When Moses was leading Israel through the Transjor-
danian region on the way to the promised land, he encountered another wicked king who, like the Pharaoh of Egypt,
tried to destroy him. This was Balak, king of Moab, who sum-
moned *from the East* (Nm 23:7) [17] a famous seer named Balaam
who was to use his arts against Moses and Israel. Balaam was a
non-Israelite, an occult visionary, a practicer of enchantment —
in short, what would have been called in Jesus' time a *magus*. [18]
He and his two servants (Nm 22:22) came; but instead of cursing Moses and Israel, he had a favorable vision of the future:

[17] The Matthean story seems to echo the Greek Septuagint [LXX] version
more closely than it echoes the Hebrew, since some of the items in Numbers
22–24 to which I call attention are found only in the Greek.

[18] In New Testament times "magi" covered a wide range of those engaged in
occult arts: astronomers, fortunetellers, priestly augurers and magicians of vary-
ing degrees of plausibility. Matthew probably thinks of astronomers.

Magi and the Star

"There shall come a man out of Israel's seed, and he shall rule many nations. . . . I see him, but not now; I behold him, but not close: *a star shall rise* from Jacob, and a man [scepter] shall come forth from Israel" (Nm 24:7, 17 — partially the Greek Septuagint: LXX).

Almost certainly this passage refers to the emergence of the Davidic monarchy:[19] it was understood that David was the star that Balaam had foreseen, the man who would be given the scepter over the United Kingdom of Judah and Israel. In later Judaism the passage was taken as a reference to the Messiah, the anointed king of Davidic descent. The passage played a role in the second century A.D. when Rabbi Aqiba hailed as Messiah the revolutionary Simon ben Kosibah, nicknamed "Bar Cochba," which by popular etymology became the "son of the star."

The Herod of Matthew's story has the features not only of the Pharaoh who tried to destroy the baby Moses by killing the male children of the Hebrews, but also of King Balak who sought to destroy Moses by means of a magus from the East. Just as Balaam saw the star of David rise, the New Testament magi saw the star of the King of the Jews at its rising.[20]

The realization that such Old Testament imagery lies behind the Matthean story of the magi and the star[21] was one of the positive results of the second stage of scholarship I described in the Introduction. But now I wish to concentrate on how Matthew used this story in chapter two of his Gospel to describe the aftermath of the revelation of who Jesus is — the good

[19] The Book of Numbers was composed after the emergence of the Davidic dynasty, and so it is difficult to be sure how much is *post factum* in the oracle of Balaam.

[20] In the translation of Matthew 2:2, "at its rising" is preferable to "in the East."

[21] In a more technical discussion I would spell out the arguments for the thesis that some of what is in Matthew 1–2 came to the evangelist already shaped into stories which he combined and modified.

First Christmas Story

news which Matthew has attached to the annunciation of the conception of Jesus in chapter one. I have said above that this aftermath or sequence normally consisted of the *proclamation* of the good news to Jews and Gentiles, with the consequent twofold *response* of acceptance and rejection. The story of the magi and the star becomes for Matthew the anticipation of the fate of the good news of salvation, a fate that he knew in the aftermath of the resurrection.

First, the christological good news draws believers, and those believers, the magi, are Gentiles.[22] Yet the evangelist is Jewish enough to continue the tradition that, deprived of the Scriptures, the Gentiles never had so explicit a revelation as was given to the Jews. It was through nature that God revealed himself to the Gentiles (see Rm 1:19–20; 2:14–15), and so Matthew shows the magi receiving a revelation through astrology: the birth star associated with the King of the Jews brings them the good news of salvation. This is an imperfect revelation; for while it tells them of the birth, it does not tell them where they can find the King of the Jews. The ultimate secret of his whereabouts is locked in the special revelation of God to Israel, in the Scriptures (Mt 2:2–6). The Gentiles come to worship, but they must learn from the Jews the history of salvation. Then Matthew highlights the paradox: those who have the Scriptures and can see plainly what the prophets have said are not willing to worship the newborn king. To the contrary, the king and the chief priests and the scribes conspire against the Messiah,[23] and the wicked king decrees his death. But God spares Jesus and ultimately brings back his Son from another land (2:15).

In other words, stories reflecting Old Testament reminis-

[22] Matthew writes his Gospel from a vantage point in time when his church has become predominantly Gentile. He knows that Jesus confined himself to Israel (10:5–6; 15:24), but he expands the parable of the wicked tenants to allow for a transfer of attention to the Gentiles (21:43; no parallel in Mark and Luke).

[23] Although Matthew 2:4–6 describes the chief priests and scribes as consulting the Scriptures, the plural in Matthew 2:20 would seem to join them with Herod in the plot against the newborn king.

Magi and the Star

cences of Joseph, Moses and Balaam have now been worked into a unified anticipation of the passion and resurrection narrative. The same cast of characters is present: the secular ruler, the chief priests and the scribes are all aligned against Jesus, who has only God on his side. But God makes Jesus victorious by bringing him back. And in this process, those who have the Scriptures reject Jesus, while Gentiles come and, with the help of the Scriptures, find and adore him.

The Matthean infancy story is not only gospel (the good news of salvation) — it is the essential gospel story in miniature. And so, when we look back at the history of Christianity, perhaps we can understand better now why this infancy narrative has been one of the most popular sections of the whole Jesus story, one of the best known and of worldwide appeal. This was due not only to the appreciation of a good story that was satisfying to emotion and sentiment; it also reflected a Christian instinct recognizing therein the essence of the good news — that is, that God has made himself present to us (Emmanuel) in the life of one who walked on this earth, indeed, so truly present that this one, Jesus, was his Son. This revelation was an offense and contradiction to some, but salvation to those who had eyes to see. Of the latter the magi are truly the forerunners, the anticipation of all those who would come to worship the risen Jesus proclaimed by the apostles. The Book of Numbers presented Balaam as one from the East who could say, "I see him, but not now," since the star would not rise from Jacob until David's time. So also the Matthean magi, in seeing the star of the King of the Jews at its rising,[24] see (but not now) the one whose kingship would not be visible historically until he had hung on the cross beneath the title *The King of the Jews* and would not be communicable until he had been elevated to God's right hand through the resurrection.

[24] See note 20 above.

First Christmas Story

14

The Second Christmas Story (Luke 2:1–40)

Part I (2:1–21):
The Meaning of the Manger;
the Significance of the Shepherds

Let me emphasize that here again I am confining myself to a
portion of the *second* chapter of the Gospel, the portion that
narrates with remarkable brevity the birth of Jesus at
Bethlehem and the events that surrounded it. It is possible to
concentrate on the second chapter thus because nothing in
Luke 2:1–40 (or in Mt 2:1–21) presupposes anything that happened in chapter one. The reader can test this by reading
2:1–40 and seeing how self-understandable the narrative is,
even to the point of reintroducing and identifying Joseph and
Mary as if nothing had been said of them previously. This has
led many to argue that the material in Luke 2 was originally
independent of the material in Luke 1, even as the Matthean
story of the magi was probably once independent of the Matthean story of the dream visions of Joseph.

But if one leaves aside the question of origins and concen-
trates on the existing structure, the parallel patterns in Luke
and Matthew are striking despite the very different story lines.
In both Gospels chapter one tells of an annunciation to one
parent (to Joseph in Matthew; to Mary in Luke): an annunciation in which an angel of the Lord reveals the forthcoming
birth of the child who will be the Messiah. Then in chapter
two, after a brief reference to the birth of that child at
Bethlehem, the story focuses in each Gospel upon the divine
proclamation of the messianic birth to an audience. In Matthew
the proclamation is to Gentile magi; in Luke it is to Jewish
shepherds. Each group is guided by the revelation to come to

Manger and Shepherds

15

Bethlehem, and there they find the child with the parent(s). The magi pay him homage and bring gifts; the shepherds praise God for all they have seen and heard. Then they both return to whence they came.

This similar structural pattern in two very different stories is quite intelligible if one recognizes that the same "backwards" christological development described in the Introduction underlies both. In both Matthew and Luke the christological insight of Jesus' identity as God's Son has been moved back from the resurrection to the conception and birth. Moreover, the aftermath of that christological revelation has also been retro-
· verted. Historically, when the good news was revealed through the resurrection, there was a sequence: it was proclaimed by preachers, and some of those who heard the proclamation believed and worshiped. So also in the second chapters of Matthew and Luke there is a proclamation of the christology revealed in chapter one. It is a proclamation by a star to the magi and by an angel to the shepherds; and both shepherds and magi believe and worship.[25] Even the departure of the shepherds and the magi is dictated by the logic of christological revelation. The two evangelists know that, when the public ministry of Jesus began, there was no surrounding chorus of adoring believers, treasuring the memories of the marvels that surrounded the birth at Bethlehem. And so these forerunners of the later Christian believers have to be removed from the scene. The magi "went away to their own country," and the shepherds "returned" to their fields.

If the birth narratives of Matthew and Luke share the same christology, they also share the tendency to dramatize that christology against a background of the Old Testament, mixed

[25] In Christian history there is also a negative reaction to the proclamation, i.e., of those who refuse to believe and then seek to destroy. In Matthew's infancy narrative these are represented by Herod, the chief priests, and the scribes; in Luke's infancy narrative it is prophesied that the child is set for the *fall* and rise of many in Israel and for a sign to be contradicted (2:34).

Second Christmas Story I

in with an anticipation of Jesus' ministry. Let me show how Luke does this in 2:1–20.

The center of the narrative is the proclamation to the shepherds and their reaction, and Luke introduces this in two steps. In verses 1–5 he tells us of a census which brings Joseph and Mary to Bethlehem; and in verses 6–7 he tells us that while they were there, Mary gave birth to Jesus, swaddled him, and laid him in a manger.

Luke needs the story of the census because he believes that Mary and Joseph lived in Nazareth ("their own city," according to 2:39), and so he has to explain what they were doing in Bethlehem. (Matthew's problem was just the opposite: he pictured Mary and Joseph living in a house in Bethlehem [2:11], and he had to explain why they moved to Nazareth, instead of returning from Egypt to Bethlehem [2:22–23].) There are formidable historical difficulties about every facet of Luke's description and dating of the Quirinius census, and most critical scholars acknowledge a confusion and misdating on Luke's part.[26] Such a confusion would offer no difficulty to Catholics, since Vatican II made it clear that what the Scriptures teach without error is the truth intended by God for the sake of our salvation,[27] and that scarcely includes the exact date of a Roman census. But, faithful to the purpose of this article, let us concentrate on the theological wealth that can be drawn from Luke's description of the census.

Luke speaks of an edict that went out from Augustus Caesar

[26] Minor difficulties are that there was no single census of the whole Roman Empire under Augustus, and that there is no evidence that Roman censuses required one to go to one's place of ancestry (unless one had property there). More serious is Luke's connection between the reign of Herod the Great (1:5) and the census under Quirinius. Herod died in 4 B.C.; Quirinius became governor in Syria and conducted the first Roman census of Judea in A.D. 6–7 — and notice it was a census of Judea, not of Galilee as Luke assumes. In Acts 5:37 Luke mistakenly mentions the revolt of Judas the Galilean (provoked by the census of Quirinius) after the revolt of Theudas which occurred in A.D. 44–46. See my commentary, *The Birth of The Messiah*, for detail.

[27] Dogmatic Constitution *Dei Verbum* on Divine Revelation, III, 11.

Manger and Shepherds

when Quirinius was governor of Syria. He thus gives the birth of Jesus a solemn setting, comparable to that which he would give the baptism of Jesus by John — under Tiberius Caesar when Pontius Pilate was prefect of Judea (3:1). In the instance of the baptism Luke was hinting that the ripples sent forth by the immersion of Jesus in the Jordan would ultimately begin to change the course of the Tiber. He is hinting at cosmic significance for the birth of Jesus as well. The name of Augustus would evoke memories and ideals for Luke's readers. In 29 B.C., one hundred years before Luke wrote this Gospel, Augustus had brought an end to almost a century of civil war that had ravaged the Roman realms; and at last the doors of the shrine of Janus in the Forum, thrown open in times of war, were able to be closed. The Age of Augustus was propagandized as the glorious age of pastoral rule over a world made peaceful by virtue — the fulfillment of Virgil's dreams in the *Fourth Eclogue.* In 13–9 B.C. there was erected a great altar to the peace brought about by Augustus, and this *Ara Pacis Augustae* still stands in Rome as a monument to Augustan ideals. The Greek cities of Asia Minor adopted September 23rd, the birthday of Augustus, as the first day of the New Year. He was hailed at Halicarnassus as the "savior of the whole world"; and the Priene inscription grandiosely proclaimed: "The birthday of the god marked the beginning of the good news for the world." Luke contradicts this propaganda by showing that paradoxically the edict of Augustus served to provide a setting for the birth of Jesus. Men built an altar to the *pax Augustae*, but a heavenly chorus proclaimed the *pax Christi*: "On earth peace to those favored by God" (2:14). The birthday that marked the true beginning of a new time took place not in Rome but in Bethlehem, and a counterclaim to man-made inscriptions was the heraldic cry of the angel of the Lord: "I announce to you the good news of a great joy which will be for the whole people: To you this day there is born in the city of David a Savior who is Messiah and Lord" (2:10–11).

Second Christmas Story I

18

Luke's mention of the census would also have a meaning for readers who knew Jewish history. Past censuses had been causes of catastrophe. King David ordered a census for Israel and Judah (2 Sm 24) and incurred the wrath of God in the form of a pestilence. Most recently the census of Quirinius in Judea in A.D. 6–7 had provoked the rebellion of Judas the Galilean which was the beginning of the Zealot movement. It was this ultranationalistic movement which culminated in the Jewish revolt against Rome and the disastrous destruction of Jerusalem in A.D. 70. Those evangelists who wrote after 70 were aware that Jewish revolutionary movements had "bad press" in the Roman Empire; and so Luke went out of his way in the passion account to insist that Pilate three times acknowledged Jesus' innocence of the political and revolutionary charges against him (23:4, 14, 22). Luke's picture of the census at Jesus' birth may have had the same goal. If Judas the Galilean revolted because of the Roman census under Quirinius, the parents of Jesus were obedient to it; thus even from birth Jesus was never a party to a rebellion against Rome. Instead of being a disaster for Roman-Jewish relations, the census of Quirinius, if one understood it correctly, provided the setting for the birth of a peaceful Savior who would be a revelation to the Gentiles and a glory for the people of Israel (2:32). Indeed, this was the census foretold in Psalm 87:6 where God says: [28] "In the census of the peoples, this one will be born there."

The fulfillment of the Old Testament becomes a stronger motif when Luke moves on from the census to the actual birth,

[28] The Hebrew of the psalm refers to the registering of people from various nations in Jerusalem which now becomes their spiritual home; the Septuagint refers to princes being born there; the (late) Aramaic targum speaks of a king being brought up there. I have cited the psalm according to Origen's *Quinta* or fifth Greek column, which we now suspect was an early recension of the Greek, somewhat parallel to the *kaige* revision of the Septuagint known to us through Dead Sea discoveries (see *The Jerome Biblical Commentary*, article 69, nos. 57, 60, 61). D. Barthélemy, *Les dévanciers d'Aquila* (Leiden: Brill 1963) 148, argues that Luke may have known the *Quinta* Greek version.

Manger and Shepherds

or rather to what Mary does after the birth (2:6–7). Like Matthew, Luke is laconic about the birth itself: simply, "She gave birth to a son, her first-born." What is of importance is the description which follows: "She swaddled him in strips of cloth and laid him down in a manger, since there was no place for them in the lodgings." [29] Luke will keep coming back to this description, for the angels will tell the shepherds: "This will be your sign: You will find a baby swaddled in strips of cloth and lying in a manger" (2:12). The shepherds will know that they have come to their goal when they have found "Mary and Joseph, with the baby lying in the manger" (2:16). Speculations as to why there was no room in the lodgings erroneously distract from Luke's purpose, as do homilies about the supposed heartlessness of the unmentioned innkeeper or the hardship for the impoverished parents — equally unmentioned. Luke is interested in the symbolism of the manger, and the lack of room in the lodgings may be no more than a vague surmise in order to explain the mention of a manger. This manger is not a sign of poverty but is probably meant to evoke God's complaint against Israel in Isaiah 1:3: "The ox knows its owner and the donkey knows *the manger of its lord*; but Israel has not known me, and my people have not understood me." Luke is proclaiming that the Isaian dictum has been repealed. Now, when the good news of the birth of their Lord is proclaimed to the shepherds, they go to find the baby in the manger and begin to praise God. In other words, God's people have begun to know the manger of their Lord. [30]

To modern romantics the shepherds described by Luke take

[29] It is probable that *phatnē* is better translated by "manger" than by "stall"; it is quite unclear whether *katalyma* means "the home," "the room," or "the inn."

[30] This suggestion is well defended by C. H. Giblin, *Catholic Biblical Quarterly* 29 (1967) 87–101. He suggests that Luke's reference to the lodgings echoes Jeremiah 14:8, addressed to the Lord and Savior of Israel, "Why are You like an alien in the land, like a traveler who stays in lodgings?" For Luke this dictum too is repealed, for the Lord and Savior of Israel no longer stays in lodgings.

Second Christmas Story I

on the gentleness of their flock and have even become Christmas symbols for the common man.[31] But such interests are again foreign to Luke's purpose. The basic Old Testament background seems to be the memory that David was a shepherd in the area of Bethlehem — the city Luke refers to as "the city of David." The mention of the shepherds' flock (2:8) may betray more complicated biblical reflections. The primary passage used to relate the Messiah's birth to Bethlehem is Micah 5:1(2): "And you, O Bethlehem Ephrathah, small to be among the clans of Judah, from you there will come forth for me one who is to be a ruler in Israel." In the immediate context Micah mentions Migdal Eder, the "Tower of the Flock," which he identifies with Jerusalem/Zion: "O Tower of the Flock, hill of the Daughter of Zion, to you will come back the former dominion, the kingdom of the Daughter of Zion" (4:8). Now, it is noteworthy that Luke has shifted over to Bethlehem a terminology formerly applied to Jerusalem/Zion. In 2:4 he tells us, "Joseph went up from Galilee . . . into Judea to the city of David which is called Bethlehem." Not only is the verb "go up" a standard Old Testament expression for ascent to Jerusalem, but Jerusalem is "the city of David," never Bethlehem. Has Luke also shifted over the designation "Tower of the Flock" (Migdal Eder) from Jerusalem to Bethlehem, so that Micah's promised restoration of the former kingdom and dominion has now been fulfilled in Bethlehem? This would explain the emphasis in the proclamation given to the shepherds who are pasturing their flock near Bethlehem: "To you this day there is born *in the city of David* a Savior who is Messiah and Lord" (2:11) — a proclamation to which they respond, "Let us go over *to Bethlehem* and see the event that has taken place" (2:15).

Other evidence supports this suggestion that the Lucan mention of the shepherds and their flock may be associated with

[31] Later rabbinic writings often considered shepherds as dishonest, for they grazed their flocks on other people's lands (Babylonian Talmud, *Sanhedrin* 25b).

Manger and Shepherds

21

reflection upon Bethlehem as the Tower of the Flock. The only other biblical reference to Migdal Eder, the "Tower of the Flock," besides Micah 4–5, is Genesis 35:19–21, where after Rachel has died on the way to Ephrath, that is, Bethlehem, Jacob journeys on to Migdal Eder. In his infancy narrative Matthew used both Micah 5 and Genesis 35:19 by way of reflection on the birthplace of Jesus,[32] so it is not impossible that these two passages which mention both Bethlehem and Migdal Eder were part of an earlier reflection on the Messiah — perhaps an earlier Christian reflection antedating both Matthew and Luke, or perhaps a pre-Christian Jewish reflection. In a passage that can scarcely have been borrowed from Christians, the Targum Pseudo-Jonathan[33] offers as an Aramaic translation of Genesis 35:21: "The Tower of the Flock, the place from which it will happen that the King Messiah will be revealed at the end of days."

The Lucan story has a twofold proclamation of the Messiah by angels. The first and most important is: "I announce to you good news of a great joy which will be for the whole people: To you this day there is born in the city of David a Savior who is Messiah and Lord" (2:10–11). We have seen that this proclamation echoes in its style the imperial propaganda of Augustus, but Luke has borrowed the precise titles from his accounts of early Christian preaching. In Acts 2:32, 36 Peter says that God raised Jesus and "made him both Lord and Messiah"; in Acts 5:31 he says that God exalted Jesus as "Savior." Now that the christological understanding has been moved back from the resurrection to the conception/birth, the same titles are applicable to the newborn child.

The second angelic proclamation is of a different nature; it is the canticle Gloria in Excelsis (2:13–14):

[32] Mt 2:5–6 directly cites Micah 5:1(2); and Mt 2:17–18 presupposes Gn 35:19 where Rachel dies on the road to Bethlehem.
[33] The dating of this targum is uncertain, and in its present form it may be as late as the third century A.D.

Second Christmas Story I

22

Glory in the highest heavens to God,
and on earth peace to those favored by Him.

This is one of the four poetic canticles in the Lucan infancy
narrative; like the other three (Magnificat, Benedictus, Nunc
Dimittis) its structural connection with its immediate context is
very loose.[34] A good case can be made for the thesis that Luke
added these canticles after he wrote the main body of the infancy narrative, and that they came to him already composed
from a collection of hymns sung by Jewish Christians in praise
of what God had done in the death and resurrection of Jesus.[35]
A very close parallel to the Gloria is found in the praise sung
by the disciples as Jesus enters Jerusalem to begin his passion
(Lk 19:38):

Peace in heaven
and glory in the highest heavens.

These may even be antiphonally recited lines of the same
hymn, with the heavenly host imagined as proclaiming peace
on earth, while the disciples proclaim peace in heaven. Jewish
scholars have recognized a similarity between the Gloria sung
in honor of Jesus and the Sanctus sung by the seraphim to the
Lord of Hosts in the Jerusalem Temple (Is 6:3), especially when
we realize that in Jewish prayer tradition each of three "Holies"
("holy, holy, holy") was expanded: "Holy in the highest
heavens; . . . holy on earth, etc."[36] If the Gloria resembles the
Sanctus, Luke is again shifting the focus from Jerusalem to
Bethlehem: the hosts of angels have moved from the Temple to
praise the new presence of the Lord in Bethlehem.

[34] One can omit the canticles in 1:46–55; 1:67–79; and 2:28–33 and never miss
them. This is also true of 2:13–14 if one reads "angel" rather than "angels" in
2:15, as do some Old Latin witnesses.

[35] In this thesis Luke would have added a few lines to the canticles, such as
1:48 and 1:76–77 (lines remarkably Lucan in style), in order to adapt them to
their present setting.

[36] See D. Flusser, "Sanktus und Gloria," in *Abraham unser Vater*, ed. O. Betz
et al. (Festschrift O. Michel; Leiden: Brill 1963) 129–152.

Manger and Shepherds

23

The Lucan birth scene closes with the reactions of three different participants (2:15–20). First, there are the shepherds, the main characters of the birth scene, who come and find the angelic sign verified: the infant Messiah lies in the manger. As I have explained above, they symbolize an Israel who at last recognizes its Lord; and they glorify and praise God for all they have seen and heard (2:17, 20).[37] Second, Luke introduces unexpectedly a group of hearers who are astonished at all the shepherds report (2:18). Astonishment is a standard reaction in the Gospel (see also 1:21, 63; 2:33), and it does not necessarily lead to faith. These hearers in the infancy narrative are like those in the parable of the seed who "hear the word, receive it with joy, but have no root" (Lk 8:13).

But there is one exception among the astonished hearers, and she constitutes the third participant in the scene, namely Mary who "kept with concern all these events, interpreting them in her heart" (2:19). She is not above being astonished (2:33), but her hearing is more perceptive. In the same parable of the seed she exemplifies "Those who, hearing the word, hold it fast in an honest and good heart" (8:15).[38] Luke's description of Mary keeping with concern all these events has often been misused for the implausible thesis that she narrated the infancy narrative to Luke.[39] The idea of "keeping events with concern" appears in Genesis 37:11; Daniel 4:28 (LXX); and *Testament of Levi* 6:2, not with any suggestion of eyewitness tradition, but for attempts to discover the hidden meaning behind marvelous happenings. The Lucan Mary is making a similar attempt, and Luke mentions this because Mary is the only

[37] Bystanders glorify and praise God for what they have seen and heard both in the Gospel (Lk 7:16; 13:13; 17:15; 18:45; 19:37) and in Acts (2:47; 3:8–9; 4:21; 11:18; 21:20).

[38] Mary makes her only appearance in the Lucan Gospel account of the public ministry immediately after these words (8:19–21) and is praised for hearing the word of God and doing it.

[39] The implausibility is most visible when we consider Lucan inaccuracies about the census and the customs of presentation and purification.

Second Christmas Story I

24

adult in his infancy narrative who will last into the public ministry and even into the Church. In the Gospel (8:21) she will appear with the "brothers" of Jesus among those who hear the word of God and do it, and in Acts (1:14) she will again appear with the "brothers" of Jesus as part of the believing community awaiting Pentecost. Thus Luke knows that Mary must have sought to interpret these events surrounding the birth of Jesus and ultimately have succeeded, for she became a model Christian believer.

Part II (2:22–40):
The Presentation of Jesus in the Temple

Besides constituting the gospel reading on the Feast of the Presentation (February 2), this Lucan narrative serves as the gospel for the Sunday in the octave of Christmas. The liturgical instinct is correct: the presentation scene is an intrinsic part and, indeed, the climax of the Lucan infancy narrative.

Although the Lucan story line is very different from that of the Matthean nativity scene, thematically the two stories are remarkably similar. In both Gospels the christological "good news" that Jesus is the Son of God has been attached to the conception and birth of Jesus; this good news is proclaimed by celestial intervention to a group who were not present (by a star to magi, or by an angel to shepherds); they come to Bethlehem to believe and worship; at the end they are removed from the scene, and they go back to whence they came.

Does the thematic parallel between Matthew and Luke stop with the departure of the magi and of the shepherds, or does it continue into the next scene (the second part of chapter 2 in each Gospel), that is, into the aftermath of the magi and shepherd scenes? For Matthew this aftermath involves the attempt of the wicked King Herod to kill the child Jesus; his slaughter of the male infants; the flight to Egypt; and the return after the king's death — a story clearly patterned on the attempt of the wicked Pharaoh to kill the baby Moses, and on the return of Israel from Egypt under Moses. Luke's account of the peaceful presentation of Jesus in the Jerusalem Temple where he is greeted by Simeon and Anna is obviously a very different story in content and tone,[40] and is modeled on Hannah's (Anna's) presentation of the boy Samuel in the shrine at Shiloh where he was accepted by the priest Eli (1 Sm 1–2). Yet, if one understands that the Matthean story is a passion narrative shifted to the infancy, with the king, the chief priests and the scribes aligned against Jesus (Mt 2:4; 26:27) seeking to kill him, it is noteworthy that Luke too introduces into the presentation a theme of opposition to Jesus and of persecution. Simeon identifies Jesus as a sign to be contradicted, set for the fall of many in Israel, and as the occasion for a sword passing through the soul (Lk 2:34–35). Thus again, despite the different story lines, each evangelist uses the aftermath of the birth to introduce the same passion and suffering motif. Neither is satisfied to terminate the nativity on a totally positive note with the acceptance of Jesus by magi and shepherds. Opposition must also be depicted or predicted; for that is the history of the good news as the two evangelists know it, writing some fifty years after the death of Jesus. By some the good news has been accepted, and they have come and worshiped; but by others it has been rejected and vigorously opposed, and their rejection has produced a division in Israel.

Having compared Luke to Matthew, let us turn now to reflect upon the particular message of Luke's account of the presentation (2:22–40). In discussing the nativity itself (2:1–20), I pointed out that, in order to get Joseph and Mary from Nazareth to Bethlehem, Luke had introduced the motif of the census, and that his information about the census posed severe

---

[40] From the viewpoint of history, the two infancy narratives are quite irreconcilable at this point without an extraordinary use of imagination.

Second Christmas Story II

historical problems. Similarly here, in order to get the family from Bethlehem to Jerusalem, Luke introduces the motifs of the purification and presentation, and once again this introduction presents historical difficulties. Luke seems to be confused about two different religious customs.[41] The first custom was that of the purification of the mother at the sanctuary (Temple) after the birth of a child, a purification at which she offered two young pigeons or doves (Lv 12:1–8). The second custom was that of the presentation of the first male child to the Lord, and the paying at the sanctuary of the sum of five shekels to buy him back. Imprecisely Luke seems to think that both parents needed to be purified ("their purification" in 2:22), that the child needed to be brought to Jerusalem to be presented to the Lord (2:22b–23), and that the offering of two young pigeons was related to the presentation (2:24 in sequence to 2:22b). For our purposes here let us leave aside these minor confusions[42] in order to concentrate on Luke's theological outlook.

It is clearly the presentation that captures Luke's interest since he never mentions the purification after the initial verse of the scene (2:22a). He stresses that this action in the Jerusalem Temple was according to the Law of the Lord which he mentions five times (2:22, 23, 24, 27, 39). Previously (2:21) Luke told us that Jesus was circumcised on the eighth day; now at another temporal interval ("when the time came") the parents obey the laws of purification and presentation. In his narrative of the census of Quirinius Luke portrayed Jesus' parents as obedient to a Roman edict which caused many Jews to revolt;[43] here he shows them obedient to the demands of Jewish

---

[41] It is worth repeating that Vatican Council II (Dogmatic Constitution *Dei Verbum* on Divine Revelation, III, 11) stated that the Scriptures teach without error that truth intended by God for the sake of our salvation. Exactitude about Jewish customs would scarcely come under this category of inerrancy.

[42] Their presence, however, militates against the supposition that Luke got the birth story from Mary. Mary would have known the customs; Luke, a Gentile convert (and perhaps a proselyte to Judaism), would have only a book knowledge of them.

[43] The Quirinius census provoked the rebellion of Judas the Galilean which

religious custom. In his origins Jesus was an offense neither to Rome nor to Israel. By the time that Luke writes his Gospel the Jewish leaders have rejected Jesus; but Luke insists that Jesus did not reject Judaism.

As Jesus is presented in the Temple in fulfillment of the Law, he is met by Simeon and Anna, two characters who could have stepped out of the pages of the Old Testament. Luke identifies Anna as a prophetess (2:36), and he has Simeon moved by the Spirit [44] to utter a prophecy about Jesus' future (2:34–35). Thus, added to the Law is the element of prophecy; "the Law and the prophets," as Luke describes the heritage of Israel, [45] come together to establish a context for the beginning of Jesus' career. And this takes place in the court of the Temple during the observance of a cultic duty, so that the Temple cult joins the context established by the Law and the prophets.

At an earlier level of composition it is likely that the Lucan infancy narrative came to an end with this scene in the Jerusalem Temple [46] and so was a narrative with an almost perfect inclusion or correspondence between beginning and end. The narrative had begun with the description of an upright and pious man and woman, Zechariah and Elizabeth (1:5–7) and with the proclamation in the Temple of the good news about

was the beginning of the Zealot movement against Roman rule in Judea, as we saw in the previous essay.

[44] Even as Luke mentions "the Law" three times in the consecutive verses 22, 23, 24, so he mentions the Spirit three times in the consecutive verses 25, 26, 27. It is the same prophetic Spirit which moved Zechariah (1:67).

[45] Luke 16:16; 24:27; Acts 13:15; 24:14; 26:22; 28:23.

[46] There are good reasons for supposing two stages of composition, in the second of which Luke would have added the canticles and the story of Jesus at age twelve — all of which are quite detachable. I shall show in the next essay how that story, which is of another literary genre (similar to the hidden-life stories we find in the apocrypha), is quite independent of what has gone before and implies that the parents had no previous indication of Jesus' true identity (2:48–50). The original ending of the infancy narrative was 2:39–40; when Luke added the story of the boy Jesus, he had to repeat the information in that ending by supplying a second ending in 2:51–52 — the idea of growth or progress at Nazareth was needed to serve as a transition to the ministry.

Second Christmas Story II

John the Baptist. In the original plan the narrative came to a close in the courts of the same Temple with another pious pair, Simeon and Anna, proclaiming the good news about Jesus (2:38). Just as Zechariah was filled with Holy Spirit to utter the Benedictus in honor of John the Baptist, the prophet of the Most High (1:67, 76), so Simeon is filled with the Holy Spirit (2:25, 26, 27) to utter the Nunc Dimittis in praise of Jesus, the Son of the Most High (1:32). The woman Elizabeth reacted to the good news about John the Baptist by thanking God that he had dealt with her thus (1:24–25); and when she gave birth to the child, the good news reached her neighbors (1:57–58). Similarly the woman Anna "gave thanks to God and spoke about the child [Jesus] to all those waiting for the redemption of Jerusalem" (2:38).

The key to this remarkable parallelism between Zechariah/ Elizabeth and Simeon/Anna is the fact that both pairs have their biblical foreshadowing in the dramatis personae of the story of the birth of Samuel. Zechariah and Elizabeth were patterned by Luke on the model of Samuel's parents, Elkanah and Hannah (Anna), who yearned for a child and had their prayer granted while praying in the sanctuary. Ultimately they presented that child Samuel to the Lord (1 Sm 1:25), and there at the sanctuary was the aged high priest Eli,[47] as well as women who served at the entrance.[48] Eli blessed the parents of Samuel for having presented their son to the Lord (1 Sm 2:20), even as Simeon blessed Jesus' parents. Afterwards the parents of Samuel returned to their home (1 Sm 2:20), even as Luke 2:39 tells us that the parents of Jesus, "when they had finished

[47] Eli, Zechariah and Simeon were all old men; Eli and Zechariah were high priest and priest respectively; but the *Protevangelium of James* (8:3; 24:3–4) made a high priest of Zechariah and made Simeon his successor to make the parallelism perfect for second-century Christians.

[48] The picture of these women in 1 Samuel 2:22 is not favorable, but in the Septuagint and in the Aramaic Targums of Exodus 38:8 (the only other reference to them) we are told that they fasted and prayed at the sanctuary. This may account for Luke's description of Anna who in the Temple courts "day and night worshiped God, fasting and praying" (2:37).

Presentation

all their duties according to the Law of the Lord, returned to Galilee." We are assured twice that Samuel grew in stature and favor with God and men (1 Sm 2:21, 26), even as Luke tells us that Jesus grew and became strong, filled with wisdom and favored by God (2:40).[49] And so Luke, who began his infancy narrative by portraying the birth of John the Baptist in the light of a Samuel background, closes the infancy narrative by portraying the birth of Jesus against the same background.

In order to pursue further the Lucan theology of the scene, we need to concentrate upon the words uttered by Simeon as he embraces the child Jesus in the Temple court. To him are attributed two poetic oracles: first, the Nunc Dimittis in verses 29–32; second, the oracle concerning the sign to be contradicted in verses 34–35. In introducing each oracle Luke mentions a blessing by Simeon (28, 34). A critical study of the history of composition suggests that, like the other three canticles in the infancy narrative (Magnificat, Benedictus, Gloria in Excelsis),[50] the Nunc Dimittis was added by Luke to an already extant narrative about Simeon — if it were to be omitted, that narrative would make perfect sense with verse 27 leading directly into verse 34. Be that as it may, our interest is in the final form of the scene where the oracle of the Nunc Dimittis is Simeon's blessing of God, while the second oracle is a blessing upon the parents and especially upon Mary.

The *first oracle*, the Nunc Dimittis, is spoken by one who has been "waiting for the consolation of Israel" (2:25).[51] This picture of one in Jerusalem waiting for consolation echoes the lan-

---

[49] Also 2:52. The fact that there are two growth statements in reference to Jesus (note 46 above) has an antecedent in the two Samuel growth statements.

[50] A collection of Jewish Christian hymns may be posited as Luke's source for the four canticles — a collection which may have had its distant origin in the early post-pentecostal Jerusalem community which (like Simeon and Anna) was remembered as "day by day attending the Temple" and "praising God" (Acts 2:46–47).

[51] Notice the parallel expression for Anna's audience: "Those waiting for the redemption of Jerusalem" (2:38).

Second Christmas Story II

guage of the second and third parts of Isaiah. In the Septuagint, Deutero-Isaiah (40:1) opens with the words: "Console, console my people, says your God; speak, priests, to the heart of Jerusalem, for her time of humiliation has been filled out." In Isaiah 66:12–13, a Septuagint passage which speaks of the glory of the Gentiles, we hear: "As one whom a mother consoles, so also shall I console you; and you will be consoled in Jerusalem." If the Lucan presentation of Simeon has Isaian background, it is not surprising that Simeon's Nunc Dimittis echoes the same background. Let us recall its message.

> Mighty Master, now you may let your servant depart
> in peace, since you kept your word.
> For my eyes have seen this salvation
> that you made ready in the sight of all peoples:
> a light to be a revelation to the Gentiles
> and to be a glory for your people Israel.

The themes of seeing salvation, the sight of all the peoples, a light to the Gentiles, and glory for Israel constitute almost a pastiche[52] from passages like Isaiah 40:5; 42:6; 46:13; 49:6; 52:9–10.

Theologically it is striking that the universalism of Deutero-Isaiah has been brought over into the infancy narrative. In the previous scene Luke's view was narrower, for it was proclaimed to the shepherds that the good news of the birth of the Messiah was meant for the whole people of Israel (2:10–11). But now we hear of a salvation made ready "in the sight of all peoples" — a salvation that is "to the Gentiles" as well as "for your people Israel." Simeon can depart in peace because the consolation of Israel which he awaited has come, and this consolation of Israel has proved to be a revelation to the Gentiles as well. In introducing the Gentiles into the presentation scene, Luke once more agrees with Matthew whose interest in the Gentiles was evident in the story of the magi from the East.

[52] The cento or pastiche technique of composition is a mark of the other three Lucan canticles and is characteristic of the hymnology of early Judaism, as visible in the Dead Sea Scrolls *Hodayoth* (hymns of praise).

Presentation

31

Luke speaks of "a light to be a revelation to the Gentiles"; Matthew (2:2) spoke of a star which the magi saw at its rising. True, Matthew showed that Jesus meant salvation for the obedient in Israel, since the angel promised Joseph that the child would "save his people from their sins" (Mt 1:21). But in the dramatis personae, with the important exception of Joseph, Matthew's infancy narrative concentrated on Jews who were hostile to Jesus. On the other hand, Luke has hitherto been concentrating on obedient Jews, like Zechariah, Elizabeth, the shepherds, and Simeon. Now, having mentioned Gentiles, he turns in the words of Simeon's second oracle to the many in Israel who will be disobedient.

This *second oracle*, the sign to be contradicted, is much less general than the Nunc Dimittis, which like the other canticles could refer to the work of Jesus at any time in his career. (Indeed, the reference to an accomplished salvation may once have been directed to the cross and resurrection before Luke adapted the canticles and added them here.) But the second oracle of Simeon, which was probably originally composed as part of the infancy narrative is strongly futuristic and quite appropriate to a child whose work had not yet begun:

> Behold, he is set for the fall and rise of many in Israel
> and for a sign to be contradicted —
> indeed, a sword will pass through your own soul —
> so that the inmost thoughts of many may be revealed.

The language is poetic and symbolic but also deliberate. Luke wrote "the fall and rise"; and the emphasis belongs on "fall," as we see from the second line with its reference to "a sign to be contradicted," and from the fourth line, for in the New Testament "inmost thoughts" (*dialogismoi*) are always pejorative. At the end of his life Simeon holds in his arms a child that is just beginning life. Simeon's eyes have peered into the distance and seen the salvation that the child will offer to the Gentiles and Israel alike; but, true prophet that he is, he has also seen rejection and catastrophe. Alas, the majority of Israel will reject

Second Christmas Story II

Jesus. Of course, from Luke's viewpoint this rejection is no longer future; he knows what has happened in the course of apostolic preaching. Luke ends his story of Jesus and of the Church when Paul comes to Rome, the capital of the Gentile empire. There he accepts the truth of Isaiah's prediction that this people (the Jews) would never understand. Paul's last words emphasize "that the salvation of God has been sent to the Gentiles; they will listen" (Acts 28:28).

The really obscure line in Simeon's second oracle is addressed to Mary: "A sword will pass through your own soul." Patristic interpretations of the sword run the gamut from doubt through calumnious rejection to violent death — interpretations invalidated by the fact that Luke gives us no evidence of Mary's doubting or of her being calumniated as an unfaithful wife (contrast Mt 1:18–19) or of her dying violently. But if we smile at the lack of method in such ancient suggestions, we should recognize that a similar defect is present in the most frequent current Catholic interpretation of the line, namely, that the sword of sorrow passed through Mary's soul when she stood at the foot of the cross and saw her son die. This suggestion violates an elementary canon of interpretation: the self-intelligibility of a writing. In the Lucan description of the crucifixion Mary is never mentioned as present, and the women who had followed Jesus from Galilee are portrayed as standing at a distance (23:49). The scene in which the mother of Jesus stands at the foot of the cross is found only in John (19:25–27); it involves "the disciple whom Jesus loved," a figure who appears in no other Gospel; [53] and so there is not the slightest reason to suspect that Luke's audience would have known of the scene. The key to "A sword will pass through your own soul" should lie in Luke's own Gospel, not in John's Gospel.

The language of the statement has its closest Old Testament parallel in Ezekiel 14:17 where we are told that by way of

[53] Compare, for instance, John 20:2–10 (which has the Beloved Disciple accompany Peter to the tomb) and Luke 24:12 (where only Peter is mentioned).

Presentation

judgment the Lord may say, "Let a sword pass through the land so that I may cut off man and beast." Evidently this was a well-remembered oracle, for it is quoted in the *Sibylline Oracles* (III, 316) to describe the invasion of Egypt by Antiochus Epiphanes (*ca.* 170 B.C.): "For a sword will pass through the midst of you." The image is of a selective sword of judgment, destroying some and sparing others, a sword of discrimination and not merely of punishment. This Old Testament background is perfectly in harmony with the rest of Simeon's second oracle in Luke where the child is set for the fall and rise of many in Israel. Simeon proclaims that a discriminating judgment will come upon Israel and that it will touch Mary too, as an individual Israelite.

Is there a scene in Luke's Gospel that can show how? Yes — the one scene in the Synoptic tradition where she appears in the public ministry.[54] It is the scene where the mother and brothers come seeking Jesus, only to have him reply that his eschatological family, established by the proclamation of the kingdom, consists not in physical relationship but in a relationship of obedience to the will of the Father. Clearly it is a discriminatory scene putting the demands of God above the privilege of human relationship. (It is Jesus' application to his own situation of the truth that he proclaimed for all: "Do you think that I have come to bring peace on the earth? No, I tell you, *rather division*; for henceforth in the one house they will be divided . . . father against son and son against father, mother against daughter and daughter against mother."[55]) In the Marcan form of the discriminatory scene (Mk 3:31–35), Mary fares poorly; for she and the brothers, standing outside, are sharply contrasted with the family of disciples surrounding Jesus in-

[54] Mark 3:31–35; Matthew 12:46–50; Luke 8:19–21.

[55] Luke 12:51–53 — it is interesting that in the Matthean form of that saying, which may represent better the "Q" original, Jesus says: "I have not come to bring peace *but a sword*" (Mt 10:34–36). Was this the origin of the sword imagery in Simeon's oracle? Yet the Greek word for "sword" in Matthew 10:34 differs from the word in Luke 2:35.

Second Christmas Story II

34

side.[56] But in Luke's form (8:19–21) Mary emerges as part of the eschatological family of Jesus: "My mother and my brothers are those who hear the word of God and do it" (see Acts 1:14). Mary has had to meet the same discriminatory demand as all others. If in Luke's view she has emerged successfully as part of the family of disciples, it was not because of a physical claim upon Jesus.

The interest that Luke shows in Mary's fate in Simeon's second oracle is consonant with the interest in Mary that he showed in 2:19. In the previous essay where I discussed that verse, I pointed out that the idea that Mary "kept with concern all these events, interpreting them in her heart" had no implication that she was the eyewitness source for Luke's infancy narrative. Rather, since Mary was the only adult in the infancy narrative who would last into the public ministry and even into the Church (Acts 1:14), Luke was hinting that later on she would discover the real meaning of all the marvelous happenings associated with Bethlehem. Through Simeon's oracle Luke tells us that part of this discovery will be that she too has to face the judgment implied in Jesus' proclamation. However, since Luke has already shown Mary as doing the will of God at the time of the annunciation (1:38), he suggests here that she will be a positive exception to the generally negative reaction in Israel which is the subject of Simeon's prophecy. For her Jesus will not be a sign to be contradicted but a sign to be affirmed.

If I were to draw a practical conclusion for Mariology from this interpretation of the sword of decision that passes through Mary's soul, it would be that Mary's greatness stems from the

[56] In the Marcan context the scene is preceded by the notice that "his own" had set out to seize Jesus because they thought he was beside himself (3:21). Evidently Mark associated Mary and the brothers with "his own" and judged that they did not understand Jesus; indeed in 6:4 he describes Jesus as a prophet who is not honored "among his own relatives and in his own house." Luke omits all these negative references to Mary. For further information, see R. E. Brown et al., Mary in the New Testament (New York: Paulist 1978) 51–61, 164–170.

Presentation

35

way she made that decision to become a disciple by hearing God's word and doing it. Her decision enabled God to make her "blessed among women" (1:42). A popular piety has suggested prayer to Mary on the grounds that surely Jesus listens to his mother. This stress on physical motherhood is a misunderstanding both of the Gospel and of her greatness. The physical fact of motherhood gave her no special status according to the values Jesus preached. If she is remembered as a mother in the Christian community, it is not only because her womb bore Jesus and her breasts nourished him (11:27); rather it is because she believed the Lord's word in a way that gave her a preeminent membership in his true family of disciples (1:41; 8:21).

Second Christmas Story II

The Third Christmas Story (Luke 2:41–52)

The Finding of the Boy Jesus in the Temple

Some readers may be surprised to have the finding of Jesus in the Temple designated a "Christmas story." Since Jesus is already age twelve, this is no birth narrative as were the other Christmas stories. But if the theme of the Christmas feast involves the first revelation to others of the presence of God's Son in the world, then I maintain that the finding-in-the-Temple story had exactly that purpose.

In the present sequence of the Lucan infancy narrative, the conception of God's Son was revealed to Mary by Gabriel (Lk 1:35); and the birth of Jesus the Savior, Messiah, and Lord was revealed to the shepherds by an angel (2:11). Consequently, when the boy Jesus calls God his Father (2:49 — the core of the finding-in-the-Temple story), this is scarcely the first revelation in the Lucan Gospel of the presence of God's Son in the world. However, careful scholarly investigation of the pre-Gospel history of the Lucan infancy material shows that the present sequence may not be original. Indeed, at one time the finding-in-the-Temple story may have been a narrative quite independent of the infancy sequence that now precedes it.[57]

Let me list some of the reasons for positing the original independence of this story: [a] The finding-in-the-Temple story is of a different literary genre from the Matthean and Lucan stories of the conception and birth of Jesus. In content and tone, as we shall see, it is a canonical example of those stories

[57] The most important study in English is that of B. Van Iersel in *Novum Testamentum* 4 (1960) 161–173. I give a complete bibliography in my commentary, *The Birth of the Messiah*.

of the "hidden life" of Jesus (that is, his life with his family before the ministry) which appear in apocryphal gospels dealing with Jesus' youth. The best example of these is the second-century *Infancy Gospel of Thomas*.[58] Despite the title, this apocryphal gospel does not treat Jesus' infancy but his youth. Stories are told therein of what Jesus did at ages five, six, eight, and twelve — the last mentioned being a retelling of Luke 2:41–52. [b] The story of the finding in the Temple does not fit into the Lucan diptych arrangement of the infancy narrative, namely, one diptych containing matching annunciation scenes (Gabriel's annunciation of the conception of John the Baptist carefully parallel to Gabriel's annunciation of the conception of Jesus), and a second diptych containing matching scenes of birth, circumcision, and naming (again, the one pertaining to John the Baptist parallel to the one pertaining to Jesus). This double diptych arrangement stretches from Luke 1:5 to 2:40. It begins with the description of the aged Zechariah and Elizabeth, involving Zechariah's vision in the Temple; it ends with the description of the aged Simeon and Anna, involving Simeon's vision in the Temple. The final verse (2:40) is an ideal transition to the Gospel proper and the story of the ministry: "And the child grew up and became strong, filled with wisdom and favored by God." The finding-in-the-Temple story, coming after that conclusion in 2:40, has the air of an awkward appendage and spoils the symmetry of the diptychs. [c] In terms of intelligibility, the finding-in-the-Temple story can be read without having a knowledge of what now precedes it in the Lucan sequence. In fact, the story is read more easily as an independent unit. A reader of the present sequence, who already knows that Jesus was not conceived by Joseph, will find it curious that in the finding story Joseph is included among the "parents" of Jesus (2:41, 43) and specifically called the father of Jesus (2:48). Even more curious, in the present se-

[58] The attribution to Thomas is not easy to explain unless the tradition was already in circulation that Thomas, "the Twin," was the twin brother of Jesus, a tradition not mentioned in this particular gospel, however.

Third Christmas Story

38

quence, is the failure of Mary and Joseph to understand Jesus when he refers to God as his Father (2:49–50), since they already knew that he was God's Son from angelic revelation. If the finding in the Temple was once totally independent of such previous infancy narratives, all these curiosities are explained. [d] Finally, there are at least slight indications that the Greek of the finding story is less marked by Semitisms than is the Greek of the preceding infancy narrative.

It seems probable, then, that Luke appended to his infancy narrative (which originally ended in 2:40) a once-independent story of the finding of Jesus as a youth in the Temple. Our understanding of New Testament christology may be deepened by reflecting on this story of Jesus' boyhood. In the Introduction I explained the "backwards development" of New Testament christology, tracing the revelation of who Jesus was (the Son of God) back from the resurrection to the baptism to the conception. The first two Christmas stories were written against the background of "conception christology" — in relation to the conception of Jesus an angel revealed either to Joseph (Matthew) or to Mary (Luke) who the child-to-be-born was.

But such "conception christology" was not the only possible way of moving the perception of divine sonship back from the baptism to an earlier period. One could have gone farther back to before conception, or one need not have gone so far back as conception and could have fastened on Jesus' youth as the moment of revelation. Preexistence christology (thus, implicitly, before conception) appears in the Pauline letters.[58a]

[58a] In 1 Corinthians 8:6 there is a *hint* of creational activity by Jesus Christ, but this theme is much clearer in Colossians 1:15–17. The language of Philippians 2:6–7 (being "in the form of God" — emptying and "taking the form of a servant") was once thought to be clearly incarnational; but recent writing by Protestants and Catholics alike (Talbert, Bartsch, Grelot, Murphy-O'Connor) questions a reference to preexistence. This means that the attitude of the indisputably Pauline letters (Corinthians, Philippians) is uncertain; but in the late-Pauline (60s) or in the post-Pauline period (80s — date of Colossians?) the theme of preexistence becomes clearer. This period from the 60s to the

Finding in the Temple

But among the Gospels it is only John who follows this route and centers his pre-ministry christology on the *preexistence* of the Word before creation (Jn 1:1), thus jumping over the conception and birth of Jesus which he never mentions.[59] I would suggest that the *"hidden life"* stories follow the second route of pre-ministry christology. They have not concerned themselves with something so remote as Jesus' conception and birth but are centered on the first moments of his rational life when he himself could express a self-evaluation. In the conception stories the revelation of Jesus as God's Son had to be placed on the lips of an "angel of the Lord"; in the hidden life stories Jesus can speak and make his own revelation.

In discussing boyhood stories as a vehicle of christology, let us consider more carefully the literary genre. Anyone who studies the birth narratives in Matthew 2:1–23 and Luke 2:1–40 must be aware of the literary genre of the birth narratives of other biblical figures, for example, of Moses, of Samson, and of Samuel, which influenced the shaping of the birth story of Jesus. Similarly, when we study a narrative of Jesus' boyhood, we find analogies in the boyhood stories of other figures. In world literature there are stories about great men who already

90s would also cover the span of Johannine composition (final Gospel in the 90s), although the Johannine theme of preexistence represents an "advance" over the Pauline theme in two ways: [a] The Johannine Word is not a creature — compare Colossians 1:16; [b] Preexistence is historicized in a Gospel about the earthly Jesus (John 17:5), rather than simply appearing in poetic hymns of wisdom derivation.

[59] The preexistence christology of John and the conception christology of Matthew/Luke are two *different* Christian answers to the question of pre-ministry christology. There is not a word in John about the virginal conception of Jesus; and there is not a word in Matthew or Luke about preexistence or about incarnation (which logically presupposes preexistence). The attempt of Manuel Miguens, *The Virgin Birth* (Westminster, Md.: Christian Classics 1975) to find references to the virginal conception outside the Matthean and Lucan infancy narratives is a total failure, as recognized by reviewers in *Catholic Biblical Quarterly* 28 (1976) 576–577 ("the exegesis is faulty and the polemic wide of the mark") and in *Theological Studies* 38 (1977) 160–162 ("an uncautious book which is bound to mislead many naive readers").

Third Christmas Story

at an age between ten and fourteen showed astounding knowledge, for example, legends about the Buddha in India, Osiris in Egypt, Cyrus the Great in Persia, Alexander the Great in Greece, and Augustus in Rome. Within the Jewish background, Josephus (*Life* 2 [#9]) reports this of himself: "While still a boy about fourteen years old, I won universal applause for my love of letters, with the result that the chief priests and leading men of the city used to come to me constantly for precise information on some particulars in our ordinances." At a later age Eliezer ben Hyrcanus ran away from home; and when he was found by his father, he was studying the Law. The Jewish legends of Moses which are contemporary with the New Testament attribute to him extraordinary knowledge as a boy; they comment on how God gave him understanding and stature and beauty of appearance. (Incidentally, the reflections on Moses as a boy are placed by Philo between the birth story of Moses and the well-known ministry story — this is the same procedure I am positing for Luke who inserted a boyhood story between an infancy story which he had already composed and an account of the ministry which he had borrowed from Mark and reshaped.) In treating Samuel, Josephus (*Antiquities* V, x, 4 [#348]) tells us that the boy began to act as a prophet at the completion of his twelfth year, thus supplying a date for the call of Samuel by God in the Temple (1 Sm 3:1–18). In the Septuagint Greek story of Susanna (v. 45), Daniel as a youth ("of twelve," according to the Syro-Hexaplar version) receives a spirit of "understanding" that makes him wiser than the elders (see also v. 63). I am not suggesting that the Lucan story of Jesus' boyhood was borrowed directly from any of these examples, but simply that there was a clear pattern of boyhood stories of famous figures at about age twelve which explains why and how a boyhood story about Jesus would have been fashioned. And the Moses and Samuel examples explain why a story of Jesus' boyhood could have been attached to an infancy narrative as a preparation for his ministry.

Finding in the Temple

We must also compare the Lucan story to the apocryphal accounts of Jesus' boyhood in the *Infancy Gospel of Thomas*. Too
often those accounts are facilely dismissed as fantastic without
a real analysis of their function and origin. By concentrating on
the magical element in a story of the five-year-old Jesus making
birds out of clay, one may neglect the real point of the story,
namely, that in so doing the child Jesus provoked the charge of
violating the Sabbath (*Thomas* 2:3). Thus, there is anticipated in
Jesus' youth the drama of Sabbath violation and of Jesus'
sovereignty over against the Law. Again, if one finds repulsive
a story in which the boy Jesus caused the son of Annas the
scribe to wither up like a tree and bear no fruit (*Thomas* 3:2),
one may wrongly overlook the parallel to hostility during the
ministry between Jesus and the scribes, and between Jesus and
Annas the priest, and the further parallel to the cursing of the
fig tree. The villagers of Jesus' youth react to his childhood dis-
plays by asking, "From where does this child come, since his
every word is an accomplished deed?" (*Thomas* 4:1) — a reaction that anticipates the amazement of the citizens of Nazareth
about the adult Jesus' teaching and his mighty works. In other
words, in the *Infancy Gospel of Thomas* the unknown period of
Jesus' boyhood has been filled in by an imaginative use of what
was known about him from the accounts of the ministry. The
underlying justifying principle is that the child must already
have been what the man was known to be, that is, God's Son
speaking and acting with divine power. I contend that the
same christological instinct has been at work in the Lucan story
of the finding of Jesus in the Temple.[60] In this story Jesus has
already begun his activity in the Temple, an activity that will
mark the culmination of his public ministry (Lk 19:45–48). As a
boy Jesus already places priority on the demands of God over
the demands of family, as he will do again during the ministry
(Lk 8:21). And his first words are to proclaim that God is his

[60] The author of the *Infancy Gospel of Thomas* recognized kindred material in
the Lucan story of the finding in the Temple, for he chose an adaptation of it to
end his sequence of hidden-life stories (19:1–5).

Third Christmas Story

Father, anticipating the heavenly voice at the baptism (Lk 3:22).

In the general pattern of boyhood stories there is customarily stress on at least three features anticipated from what is known of the subject's later career: his piety, his wisdom, and some distinctive aspect of his life work. If we examine in detail the Lucan story of the finding of the boy Jesus in the Temple, we shall find those three features present in an ascending order of importance. To facilitate this discussion let me suggest the following outline for Luke 2:40–52:[61]

> Framework Statement about Jesus' growth, his wisdom and
> favor (40)
> Geographical Introduction: Jesus and his parents had gone
> up to Jerusalem (41–42)
> Setting: The parents lost Jesus and searched for him
> (43–45)
> Core of the Story: The parents found the child and were
> amazed; Jesus answered them by stressing his
> Father's claim (45–50)
> Geographical Conclusion: Jesus went down with his parents
> to Nazareth (51)
> Framework Statement about Jesus' progress in wisdom, matu-
> rity, and favor (52)

Luke first calls attention to the piety of Jesus and his family. This is harmonious with the picture he has painted throughout the birth narrative; for he described the parents going to Bethlehem in obedience to the edict of Caesar Augustus (2:1, 4), naming the child Jesus in obedience to the angel (2:21), and going to the Jerusalem Temple in obedience to the Law of

[61] Verse 40 of chapter 2 was, in my theory, the original ending of the Lucan infancy narrative providing a transition to the ministry. When Luke added the finding-in-the-Temple story, he supplied another ending-verse transitional to the ministry (v. 52). The presence of these two statements about Jesus' growth is another indication that the finding story is an appendage.

Finding in the Temple

Moses about purification and presentation (2:22–24). In the finding story the parents are again obedient to the Law by going up to Jerusalem for the Feast of Passover (2:41).[62] But Luke adds here implicitly a new note, for Jesus is also respectful of duty and is pious in accompanying his parents on the Temple visit to Jerusalem.[63] We are in the same context of "Temple piety" that marks the Lucan description of the first Christians in the Book of Acts (2:46; 3:1; 5:12). Thus, at the beginning of both his books, the Gospel and Acts, Luke makes it clear that the Law and the cult provided a benevolent context for Jesus. If, later on, antipathy developed between his followers and the Jewish authorities precisely over the Law and the Temple, there was no conflict between Jesus himself and the best in Judaism.

Second, Luke calls attention to the wisdom of Jesus. As it now stands, the story of the finding of Jesus in the Temple is framed by two references to Jesus' growth, one terminating the birth narrative which precedes the finding, the other leading into the ministry narrative which will follow:

2:40 "And the child grew up and became strong, filled with wisdom and favored by God."

2:52: "And Jesus made progress in wisdom, maturity [or stature: *hēlikia*], and favor before God and men."[64]

These statements are virtually a Lucan modification of the two growth descriptions in 1 Samuel.[65]

[62] Passover had now been joined to the Feast of the Unleavened Bread, and the combined feast was a "pilgrimage" feast when Jews were obliged to appear "before the Lord" in the Jerusalem Temple to worship and make an offering (Ex 23:17; 34:23; Dt 16:16).

[63] This has nothing to do with the much later custom of Bar Mitzvah. We do not know that at age twelve Jesus would have been *obliged* to go to Jerusalem; the general talmudic principle is that a child reaches manhood at his thirteenth birthday.

[64] Compare the description of the boy Moses in Josephus, *Antiquities* II, ix, 6 [#230]: "His growth in understanding was not proportionate to his growth in stature [*hēlikia*] but far outran the measure of his years."

[65] In my previous essay on the presentation I showed how closely the Lucan

Third Christmas Story

44

2:21: "And the child [Samuel] waxed mighty before the Lord.

2:26 "The child advanced and was good in the company of God and men."

The reason why Luke mentions wisdom in both the growth statements which supply a framework for the narrative becomes apparent as we move into the core of the story. Jesus is found in the Temple listening to the teachers and asking them questions; and we are told: "All who heard him were astounded at his understanding and his answers." Clearly here we have anticipated on the boyhood level the kind of amazement at the teaching of Jesus that will mark his ministry. This scenario is presented by an evangelist who already knew the later scene at Nazareth when, after Jesus spoke in the synagogue, all "wondered at the gracious words that proceeded out of his mouth" (Lk 4:22), and the scene in another synagogue when people were amazed at Jesus' authoritative words (4:36), and finally the scene in the Temple near the end of his life where Jesus taught before the chief priests and the scribes (19:47).[66] The boy Jesus is already showing the wisdom in sacred teaching which will mark his career as a man, and the people are reacting in the same way they will react during the ministry.

The *third* Lucan motif, besides piety and wisdom, is a boyhood anticipation of a basic attitude of Jesus' life. I have already noted that, while the apocryphal boyhood stories anticipate the themes of Jesus' ministry, they allow an admixture of the marvelous to dominate their presentations. If the finding-in-the-Temple story were preserved only in an apocryphal

account of the infancy of Jesus follows the Old Testament account of the infancy of Samuel.

[66] In the ministry scene the chief priests and scribes are hostile to the teaching of Jesus, but in the boyhood story Luke does not surround Jesus with any hostility on the part of the teachers in the Temple — perhaps that is why Luke prefers here to call them "teachers" rather than "scribes," a term that might evoke hostility in the minds of his readers.

Finding in the Temple

gospel, we can be sure that the amazement over Jesus' teaching would be greatly enlarged.[67] But Luke wisely makes the theme of Jesus' wisdom subordinate to a dialogue between Jesus and his parents (2:48–49). The question asked by Jesus' mother ("Child, why have you done this to us? Behold your father and I have been so worried looking for you") has a slight tone of reproach, a tone better understood if one posits that this was once an independent story without a preceding narrative of angelic visions to Mary. The atmosphere is not unlike that of the first scene involving Jesus and his mother in Mark. According to Mark 3:21, when "his own" heard about his all-consuming ministerial activity, "they set out to seize him." This is preparatory for 3:31: "And his mother and his brothers came; and standing outside, they sent to him and called him." Similarly, too, in the first conversation between Jesus and his mother reported in the Fourth Gospel (Jn 2:3), the mother lays upon Jesus a type of family claim in reporting that her friends (or, perhaps, relatives) are out of wine. In all these scenes where a demand is placed on Jesus in the name of family obligations, his response shows that his priorities are with God rather than with earthly family. And so in Luke 2:49 he responds to his parents, "Why were you looking for me? Did you not know that I must be in my Father's house?" In Mark 3:33–34, to the demand of his mother and brothers, Jesus says: "Who are my mother and my brothers? . . . Whoever does the will of God is my brother and sister and mother." In John 2:4 Jesus replies to his mother's request, "Woman, what has this concern of yours to do with me? My hour has not yet come" — priority is given to the "hour" of Jesus determined by his rela-

[67] In the apocryphal version of the finding story in the *Infancy Gospel of Thomas* we hear: "All paid attention to him and were astounded how he, a child, put to silence the elders and teachers of the people, expounding sections of the Law and the sayings of the prophets" (19:2); and the scribes ask Mary in wonder: "Are you the mother of this child? . . . Never have we seen or heard such glory and such excellence and wisdom" (19:2, 4).

Third Christmas Story

46

tion to the heavenly Father (13:1). The three Gospels have different wording but the same import.

Thus the dialogue between Jesus and his parents brings a real gospel motif into the story of the finding in the Temple. Moreover, in stressing the priority of God's claim, Jesus refers to God as his Father: "Did you not know that I must be in my Father's house?" [68] This reference makes the finding story a vehicle of self-revelation: Jesus is acknowledging that he is God's Son. The christological revelation, which we discussed above, has been moved back to the first moment of Jesus' adulthood.

Let me pause here to make a parenthetical remark about the implications of modern biblical criticism for this scene: the scene teaches us *nothing* about the historical development of Jesus' self-knowledge. Conservative interpreters have argued on the basis of 2:49 that already as a boy Jesus knew that he was the Son of God; liberal interpreters have argued from 2:52 ("Jesus made progress in wisdom") that as a boy Jesus did not know all things. Neither argument respects the nature of this story. The statement that we hear in 2:49 on the lips of Jesus represents the God-given insight of the post-resurrectional Christian community that Jesus is the Son of God. The statement about Jesus' progress in 2:52 is a stereotyped imitation of similar Old Testament growth statements, for example, those referring to Samuel. What one can legitimately infer from the respective verses is that *Luke's appreciation* of Jesus did not cause him any difficulty in stating that Jesus grew in wisdom and God's favor, and that *Lucan christology* did not hesitate to

[68] The Greek of Luke 2:49 is ambiguous; literally the key phrase is "in the . . . of my Father," with the plural of the definite article used in place of a noun. The suggestion that Luke means "in the dwelling-place (house) of my Father" is slightly more probable than the suggestion that he means "in or about the things (business, affairs) of my Father." However, since the word "house" is not used but at most implied, there is no stress on the identity of the Temple as the house of God, a stress falsely placed by some commentators.

Finding in the Temple

affirm that Jesus was God's Son even before the baptism in the Jordan.[69]

Returning to the Lucan story, we find that Jesus' reference to his Father is not understood by his parents (2:50). In the pre-Lucan form of the story their lack of understanding offered no problem because this was probably the first revelation of Jesus' identity. In the present Lucan sequence where the parents already know that Jesus is God's Son,[70] the lack of understanding centers not on his identity but on the priority that he gives to the claims of his vocation over the claims of his parents. Particular Lucan attention is given to Mary, the one adult from these infancy and youth stories who will continue into the account of the ministry. Only later will she come to understand the true nature of Jesus' family. In Luke 8:19–21, when Mary and the brothers come asking for Jesus, Jesus will finally make

[69] Although I have already written on the issue in *Jesus God and Man* (Macmillan paperback edition, 1972) 79–102, may I be allowed to repeat that the question "When did Jesus find out that he was God?" makes little sense (even as the liberal affirmation "Jesus did not know that he was God" makes less sense). This question is usually asked by a Christian who is presupposing a trinitarian conception of God, phrased in the categories of Greek philosophy of the fourth century, to test the human knowledge of a Galilean Jew of the first century in whose language "God" would mean the Father in heaven. If the question is phrased more intelligently, "When did Jesus come to understand his unique relationship to God?" — a uniqueness that *we* have rightly come to phrase in terms of divinity — then the question is not answerable biblically. Moreover, it is probably no more answerable psychologically than the question of when we come to understand that we are human. To a certain extent people understand who they are from the first moment they can think, even though it may take a lifetime to phrase that inchoative understanding adequately. By psychological analogy, if Jesus was God's Son (as we believe), he should have had some human awareness of his uniqueness from the first moment he could think, even though he never had the Greek philosophical language of the fourth century to phrase his self-understanding. But then is psychological analogy valid in the instance of Jesus?

[70] Note the climactic arrangement pertinent to Jesus' identity in the existing Lucan narrative: in chap. 1 an angel proclaims that Jesus is God's Son; in chap. 2 Jesus proclaims it; in chap. 3 God the Father will proclaim it at the baptism.

Third Christmas Story

48

clear that their importance is based not on physical relationship but on obedience to God: "My mother and my brothers are those who hear the word of God and do it." But Mary cannot understand that before the ministry, and so here Luke tells us: "His mother kept with concern all these events in her heart."[71] She is like the good disciple in the parable of the sower and the seed, where the seed that falls on good soil stands for "those who, hearing the word of God, hold it fast in an honest and good heart, and bring forth fruit with patience" (Lk 8:15).

At the end of the finding story (2:51) Luke wrestles with a problem that faces all pre-ministry tales. If the revelation of Jesus' identity is already given long before the baptism (whether at birth or in boyhood), why is it that people do not know who he is when he begins his ministry? In the birth stories Matthew and Luke handle this difficulty by specifying that those who received the revelation (the magi or the shepherds) left the scene and returned to whence they came (compare Mt 2:12 and Lk 2:20). But in this boyhood story the problem is complicated by the fact that Jesus himself has made the revelation and has begun to show his wisdom. If Jesus should continue behaving in this way, how will Luke plausibly describe a situation where the people at Nazareth will have no suspicion that Jesus is God's Son and think that he is merely Joseph's son (Lk 4:22)? To avoid such a conflict Luke insists on the uniqueness of this moment of self-assertion by Jesus. His normal pattern at Nazareth was to be obedient to his parents: "He went back down with them to Nazareth and was obedient to them" (2:51). And so Jesus gave the people at Nazareth no reason to suspect that God was his Father. In Mark's Gospel Jesus is the Son of God during the ministry, but his followers

---

[71] I have been suggesting that functionally the revelation by the boy Jesus in the finding story is the same as the revelation by an angel in the earlier Lucan infancy account. It is not surprising, then, that Luke's description of Mary's reaction here echoes his earlier description of Mary's reaction to the revelation following Jesus' birth: "Mary kept with concern all these events, interpreting them in her heart" (2:19).

Finding in the Temple

49

do not know it because he hides his power from them. Luke has moved the Marcan Secret back to the boyhood of Jesus. The poignancy that God's Son should willingly subject himself to obedience anticipates a fundamental tension of the ministry. Here Luke is remarkably close to Hebrews 5:8: "Although he was a Son, he learned obedience." The last of the Christmas stories proclaims the good news that God's Son is already in the world, but it also foreshadows the cross by insisting that Jesus preserved his identity in the role of a servant.

Third Christmas Story